CLIFTON PARK-HALFMOON PUBLIC LIBRARY

W9-DGV-390

CLIFTON PARK-HALFMOON PUBLIC LIBRARY

BUILT FOR SUCCESS

THE STORY OF

Amazon.com

Published by Creative Education
P.O. Box 227, Mankato, Minnesota 56002
Creative Education is an imprint of The Creative Company
www.thecreativecompany.us

DESIGN BY **ZENO DESIGN**
PRODUCTION BY **CHRISTINE VANDERBEEK**
ART DIRECTION BY **RITA MARSHALL**

Printed by Corporate Graphics in the United States of America

PHOTOGRAPHS BY Alamy (Lynne Sutherland, Kristoffer
Tripplaar), Corbis (Dan Lamont, Tim Wimborne/Reuters), Getty
Images (Kevin P. Casey/Bloomberg, Tim Boyle, Ken James/
Bloomberg, Joshua Lott/Bloomberg, Charles Ommanney,
Spencer Platt, Space Frontiers, Thinkstock, Rex Rystedt/
Time Life Pictures, Chris Ratcliffe/Bloomberg, Kevin Schafer,
Brendan Smialowski, Justin Sullivan, Sabastian Willnow/AFP)

Copyright © 2013 Creative Education
International copyright reserved in all countries. No part of
this book may be reproduced in any form without written
permission from the publisher.

Amazon.com® and the products discussed in this book are
either trademarks or registered trademarks of Amazon.com,
Inc. Trademarks associated with products of other companies
mentioned are the trademarks of their respective owners.
This is not an official publication of Amazon.com, Inc., and the
views set out herein are solely those of the author.

LIBRARY OF CONGRESS CATALOGING-IN-PUBLICATION DATA

Gilbert, Sara.
The story of Amazon.com / by Sara Gilbert.
p. cm. — (Built for success)
Summary: A look at the origins, leaders, growth, and products
of Amazon.com, the electronic commerce company that was
founded in 1994 and today is the largest online retailer in the
United States.
Includes bibliographical references and index.
ISBN 978-1-60818-174-2
1. Amazon.com (Firm)—History—Juvenile literature. 2. Internet
bookstores—United States—Juvenile literature. 3. Electronic
commerce—United States—Juvenile literature. 4. Bezos,
Jeffrey—Juvenile literature. I. Title.

Z473.A485G55 2012   5831
381'.4500202854678—dc23   2011035747

CPSIA: 112612 PO1620

9 8 7 6 5 4 3 2

BUILT FOR SUCCESS

THE STORY OF

Amazon.com

SARA GILBERT

Clifton Park - Halfmoon Public Library
475 Moe Road
Clifton Park, New York 12065

S hortly after the Amazon.com Web site launched on July 16, 1995, a loud beep echoed through the company's offices near downtown Seattle. The beep alerted the Amazon.com staff that the first customer had made a purchase, ordering a copy of the book *Fluid Concepts and Creative Analogies: Computer Models of the Fundamental Mechanisms of Thought* by Douglas Hofstadter. The beep sounded six more times that day and was accompanied each time by a raucous cheer from Amazon employees. But those beeps quickly became more frequent—and more distracting to the small staff—as the company logged more than $12,000 worth of purchases in its first week. As Amazon prepared for a continued onslaught of orders, the beeping sound was deemed too annoying, and the function was disabled.

CHAPTER ONE

Settling in Seattle

The moving van filled with all of Jeff Bezos's belongings had left New York City on a summer morning in 1994 and driven westward for almost 24 hours before Bezos called to designate a final destination. Bezos had left his job as senior vice president at a prominent New York investment company to start a business of his own—but he wasn't quite sure where.

A day after giving up the Manhattan apartment he shared with his wife, Mackenzie, he made his decision. He called the movers, loaded a battered 1988 Chevrolet Blazer, and headed to Seattle, Washington.

While Mackenzie drove, Bezos spent the time it took to cross the country working on a rough business plan for the Internet-based bookstore he had spent months researching. He saw enormous potential for growth in the Internet and the World Wide Web, which had only begun to be used by the general public in the fall of 1993. By the spring of 1994, hundreds of thousands of people were already using the Web—and usage was growing at an incredible rate of 2,300 percent per year. "Things don't grow that fast outside of petri dishes," Bezos said. At that rate, he believed that the Internet could be "invisible today and ubiquitous [everywhere] tomorrow."

Seattle is known for its numerous technology companies, frequent rain, and iconic Space Needle

AMAZON.COM

Bezos knew that he had to build his Web-based business quickly, before every other **entrepreneur** in the world figured out the Web's potential to reach consumers as well. He chose books as his business because they were an almost universal product, with more than three million titles available worldwide. Books were relatively easy to acquire, either directly from publishers or from one of the large distributors already supplying **brick-and-mortar** bookstores. He also knew that individual books were reasonably priced, making them affordable to most people. And Bezos was confident that building his bookstore on the Web, without the costs of maintaining a physical store, would enable him to cut prices more deeply than traditional booksellers could.

Seattle's proximity to one of the largest book distribution centers—Ingram Book Group, in nearby Roseburg, Oregon—played a role in Bezos's decision to move there. Seattle was also gaining prominence as a high-tech city, with such businesses as Microsoft, Nintendo, and other **software** development firms nearby, making it a great place to find talented computer **engineers**.

When Bezos started looking for a home to rent in Seattle, he had one primary requirement: It needed a garage. Many of his entrepreneurial heroes had started their businesses in garages, and he wanted to do the same. The house he and Mackenzie found had a one-car garage that had been converted into a family room. Although Bezos joked that it wasn't a completely legitimate garage, that's where he set up his office in November 1994. Together with the two software programmers he had recruited—Sheldon Kaphan and Paul Barton-Davis—he filled the room with file cabinets, bookshelves, a large round table, and two desktop computers. On the walls, the men hung white drawing boards on which they could create visual maps of how the Web site would work.

Then they got busy working out the technical details of the Web site, including what it would look like and how it would store information about customers' orders. Relying heavily on open-source software, which programmers write and then make available to other programmers around the world at no charge, Bezos,

Amazon was originally built around books, soon promoting itself as "the world's largest bookstore"

Kaphan, and Barton-Davis developed the framework for the online bookstore.

At the same time, Bezos consulted catalogs from publishing companies to compile a list of books available for purchase in the United States and around the world. He also tried to secure financial backing for the company, since he had been footing all the bills for the business himself. In February 1995, Bezos's father invested more than $100,000 in exchange for **stock** in the business, which was **incorporated** as Amazon.com that same month. Later that year, his mother authorized another stock purchase through a family **trust** that brought in almost $150,000.

That addition of cash was enough to hire a few more employees. It also helped move Amazon's operations out of the garage, where all the equipment had pushed the space's sole electrical **circuit breaker** to the limit, and into a larger space in Seattle's industrial district. Bezos joked that they needed access to additional outlets more than they needed additional space. "I know why people move out of garages," he said. "It's not that they run out of room, it's that they run out of electrical power."

By the time Amazon.com had moved into its new location, all software testing had been completed, and the company was ready to launch its site. On July 16, 1995, the Amazon.com Web site went live with a bold tagline typed underneath its logo: "Earth's Biggest Bookstore." The homepage invited visitors to "Search one million titles" and to "Enjoy consistently low prices."

Although the company was known primarily by word of mouth at that point, sales started trickling in immediately. Then, three days after the launch, new Web **search engine** Yahoo! placed Amazon.com on its "What's Cool" list, and the amount of traffic on the site expanded rapidly. By the end of the first week, Amazon.com had tallied $12,438 in orders.

"We see our customers as invited guests to a party, and we are the hosts. It's our job every day to make every important aspect of the customer experience a little bit better."

JEFF BEZOS, AMAZON.COM FOUNDER

Jeff Bezos went to college at Princeton University, studying computer science and electrical engineering

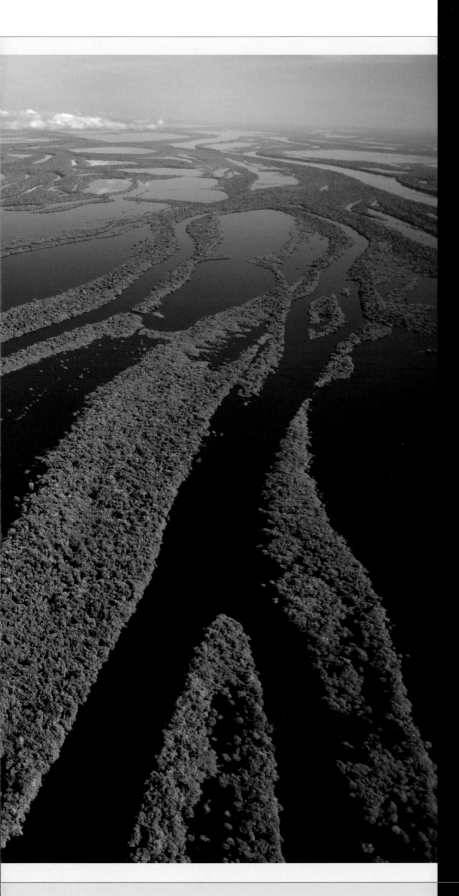

FROM MAGIC TO A RIVER

When Jeff Bezos originally incorpo
rated his company, he did so under
the name Cadabra, Inc.—a short
ened version of the magical phrase
"Abracadabra." His first clue that
he would have to change the name
came when he mentioned it over
the phone to his attorney, who mis
takenly heard Bezos say "Cadaver"
(meaning "dead body"). Aside from
that confusion, Bezos decided that
he wanted a name that started with
the letter *a* so that it would have
prominence in alphabetical listings.
He paged through the dictionary
and considered using the Old Dutch
word *aard*, which means "earth," be
cause of its alphabetical significance.
Eventually, he decided on Amazon
instead. "Jeff was really excited about
the fact that here was a river that was
10 times larger than the next biggest
river," remembered early software
programmer Paul Barton-Davis. "It's
not just big, it's so much bigger than
its next nearest competitor."

CHAPTER TWO

Getting Big Fast

Quite quickly, Amazon.com was averaging 2,200 hits, or customer visits, daily. Orders were adding up so fast that projected annual **revenue** climbed to $5 million. But even as sales figures rose, the costs of building a workforce, maintaining equipment, and developing services totaled more than what the company was making.

Bezos was broke, and his family wasn't able to invest any more money in the operation. Although Bezos was willing to wait for Amazon to make money—his original business plan had predicted that it would be five years before the company would turn a **profit**—he needed funds to remain in business.

With the help of a well-connected friend, Bezos secured $981,000 in private funding by the end of 1995. That helped the company move to a nearby two-story, 17,000-square-foot (1,580 sq m) building with a warehouse space big enough to hold the site's growing inventory of titles in March 1996. Despite gaining a total of 15,000 square feet (1,394 sq m), however, Bezos predicted that Amazon would outgrow the new building within six months.

Bezos was right, thanks in part to a glowing article about Amazon in the *Wall Street Journal* on May 16, 1996, which attracted the attention of both new customers

One of Amazon's primary challenges in its early years was maintaining sufficient warehouse space

and new investors. Venture capitalists, who fund new and emerging companies in exchange for stock, started calling Bezos, eager to be involved in the flourishing business. Amazon accepted $8 million in cash from Kleiner Perkins Caufield & Byers, a venture capital firm that had already invested in the computer services company Netscape and computer maker Compaq, in exchange for a 13 percent stake in the company.

That financial infusion made it possible for the Amazon team to start thinking even bigger. Bezos added employees—managers, warehouse workers, and customer service agents—but couldn't find adequate space for them all. Desks were set up in the kitchen area, and conferences were held in the middle of a room filled with people working. In the midst of it all were several dogs, who were welcome to join their masters at work. By August, the offices had moved again, this time to a building downtown. The warehouse remained in the same location until November, when it was moved to a 93,000-square-foot (8,640 sq m) facility in South Seattle.

Amazon's next big move was onto the publicly traded stock market. Although the company was still losing money and its biggest competitor, Barnes & Noble, was launching an online bookstore of its own, Amazon's staggering growth impressed investors. In the first **quarter** of 1997, sales soared to $16 million—more than the total for all of 1996. Those figures helped the company raise $54 million when it went public on May 15, 1997.

Sales grew so much during the rest of 1997 that by October, just two years after Amazon had launched, the one-millionth customer placed an order. Bezos flew to Japan to personally deliver the books—a computer text and a biography of Princess Diana. In November, Amazon opened a second warehouse facility in Delaware to help house up to 300,000 titles and to make it possible to ship products from both sides of the country. By the end of the year, Amazon had made $147.8 million, an 838 percent jump over the previous year. But because it was adding employees, investing in new buildings, and increasing its

Amazon rented space in Seattle's impressive Pacific Medical Center for its headquarters from 1998 to 2010

marketing expenses, the company again lost more money than it made.

As the value of Amazon.com stock climbed above $100 per **share** in the spring and summer of 1998, Bezos began expanding the site's offerings to include music and movies. He also orchestrated several **acquisitions**, including price search engine Junglee Corp., which searched for the best possible price for almost any product sold online. The acquisition was an important step in preparing the company to sell products other than books and made clear Bezos's goal to turn Amazon into a one-stop shopping site. He also successfully launched the company's first two international sites in the United Kingdom and Germany. Each site had its own in-country customer service and distribution centers to better serve Amazon's European customers.

Bezos, who had printed T-shirts for his first employee picnic with the slogan "Get Big Fast," was making sure that Amazon lived up to that goal—even if it wasn't yet making money. In 1999, Amazon opened four new fulfillment centers, in addition to a site in Tacoma, Washington, dedicated entirely to providing customer service to the company's eight million shoppers. It also continued to branch out beyond books by offering electronics, toys and board games, home improvement products, software, video games, and gifts. The company also launched an auction site intended to rival eBay, which had established itself as the dominant force in the online auction market.

Adding all of that—and maintaining a workforce of more than 5,000 employees in the U.S. and Europe—meant another year of record losses for the company. But that didn't deter the editors of *TIME* magazine, who selected Bezos as Person of the Year for 1999. In the midst of rapid growth in online businesses, the magazine described the 35-year-old Internet entrepreneur as "unquestionably, the king of cybercommerce" and lauded his efforts to help "build the foundation of our future."

"*Amazon has shown people how big the Internet can be as an economic phenomenon.*"

BUSINESS ANALYST HENRY BLODGET

Distribution centers in Germany contributed greatly to Amazon's efforts to become truly global

Jeff Bezos

DOORS FOR DESKS

When Amazon.com launched an auction site in 1999, one of the first items listed was Jeff Bezos's original desk, which was being sold to raise money for the World Wildlife Fund. Bezos had built the desk himself out of an 80-pound (36 kg), solid-core particleboard door. The door was fastened to four legs, and although it was a bit wobbly, it served Bezos's needs well. He and another employee constructed similar desks for the rest of the staff, evidence of the company's commitment to keeping costs down and passing the savings on to customers. Most of the early office furniture that wasn't built by employees was purchased from garage sales or auctions. "Jeff wanted us to put little stickers on the furniture to show how much money we saved on it," said Amazon's original **comptroller**, Gina Meyers, who admitted that the staff never followed through on that order. Bezos's desk sold for $30,100 at auction.

CHAPTER THREE

Pushing for Profits

B y early 2000, Amazon.com had become the all-encompassing shopping destination that Bezos had envisioned. Although the business was still built around books, it was now a gateway to almost anything any online shopper could desire, from health and beauty products to lawn and patio furniture and even new cars.

Most of these items were offered through other retailers, who were able to list their products on Amazon in return for a portion of the profits. An alliance with the giant kids' store Toys"R"Us connected Amazon with that company's enormous inventory of toys and other kids' merchandise as well. In spite of these additions, the company's debt was continuing to grow faster than its sales numbers, which had leveled off. At the same time, many of the Web-based businesses that had been launched during the Internet heyday in the late 1990s were failing in an **economic** shakedown that came to be known as the "dot-com bust."

All of that contributed to a growing sense of pessimism about Amazon.com's future. Stock market analysts were beginning to wonder if the business model was viable, and they questioned whether Amazon would ever turn a profit. Stockholders were complaining about the steep drop in the value of the company's shares. One

Toys"R"Us had been in business for 43 years before it partnered with Amazon in the year 2000

group had even filed a series of lawsuits against the company, alleging that they had been misled by financial information Amazon had provided them. Even the press, which had lauded Bezos for his ingenuity just a few months earlier, had turned more critical. The company was being labeled with such nicknames as "Amazon.bomb" and "Amazon.toast" as critics predicted the company's collapse. "You go from Internet poster child to Internet whipping boy," Bezos said in a *Fortune* magazine article in December 2000. "It takes like 30 seconds."

Although Bezos was known for his relaxed manner (he wore khaki pants and collared shirts without ties, even to shareholder meetings, and allowed his employees to dress in the same casual style), he suddenly felt intense pressure to show a profit, and fast. At the end of 2000, he sent an e-mail to all Amazon employees announcing the company's internal goal to turn a profit within a year. "We're aiming to have sales of $5 billion, produce over $1 billion in gross profits, and achieve solid operating profitability," Bezos wrote.

To help move in that direction, Bezos, who had always been notoriously tight about spending company dollars, cut back even further on spending in every area of the business. He laid off approximately 1,300 workers, closed 2 warehouses and a customer service center, and brought in experts to help streamline the business's processes. He also purged products that weren't profitable—including many electronics, kitchen items, and tools—from the site's offerings. Then he forged a partnership with bookstore giant Borders to foster cooperation, rather than competition, between the two businesses. Many observers considered those moves a positive sign, and some believed they would help Amazon realize a profit within two years.

By early 2001, Amazon's stock values had dropped to approximately $15 a share after climbing to $139 in 1998, and the company reported a loss of $1.4 billion—its worst performance to date. The battered Bezos started his annual letter to shareholders in April 2001 by saying, "Ouch, it's been a brutal year." But by the end of the year, Bezos had much better news to report: On the strength

By 2000, Amazon had grown well beyond books, selling an increasingly diverse array of products

of a strong holiday season, Amazon reported fourth-quarter profits of $5 mil-lion—a signal to investors that Amazon was moving in the right direction.

Amazon's next step was to further expand its product offerings and improve its customer service to woo and keep more customers. In 2002, it made free shipping—which had been introduced in 2000 on orders of more than $100—available on certain orders of at least $25 worth of products. It cut prices on many items and added office necessities, clothing, and accessories to the in-ventory available on the site. It also launched Amazon Web Services, a new venture that capitalized on the expertise the company's technical staff had developed while building and maintaining the Amazon site, to offer Web site solutions to other businesses.

The company reported a net loss of $149 million for 2002—significantly less than the $567 million it had lost the previous year. And once again, it turned a profit in the fourth quarter, thanks in part to its own efforts and in part to the rebounding economy in general. Although Amazon's stock prices were still down dramatically, the company was now being lauded as a survivor, since it was one of the few e-commerce companies still in business after the devastat-ing dot-com bust. Some financial analysts even speculated that the company might be able to show its first full-year profit in 2003.

Despite the improvements, some experts remained unconvinced that Amazon's future was stable. An article in *Business Week* magazine in the sum-mer of 2002 noted that, while the company had successfully pulled itself back from the brink of collapse, it still wasn't completely in the clear. "After seven years and more than $1 billion in losses," the article asserted, "Amazon is still a work in progress."

"Amazon was probably the first truly worldwide community that was built online."

SCOTT LIPSKY, A FORMER AMAZON EXECUTIVE

Amazon has long relied on a surge of holiday sales in December for much of its annual revenue

An Amazon distribution center

TALE OF TWO AMAZONS

In 1970, a nonprofit **feminist** bookstore opened its doors in Minneapolis, Minnesota, and called itself Amazon Bookstore. In 1999, it filed a trademark **infringement** law suit against Amazon.com, claiming that the online bookseller had used its name without permission. Amazon Bookstore had never registered its name with the U.S. Patent and Trademark Office, but it claimed that it should be protected under common law rights, which are developed through use and longevity but are not granted by law. But by the time the suit was filed, Amazon.com was already four years old and widely recognized. "Amazon Bookstore sat on its hands for four years while we were building a brand [identity]," said Amazon.com spokesperson Bill Curry. "If there was a problem they should have said something a lot sooner." To avoid a trial, Amazon settled with the bookstore out of court. Although the terms of the settlement remained private, the online company maintained rights to the name Amazon.com.

CHAPTER FOUR

Bigger and Better

Amazon's advance toward profitability continued in 2003. Customers responded to the company's price cuts and free shipping offers by placing more orders, which led to a 28 percent jump in sales during the first quarter of the year. The company, meanwhile, responded to its improved outlook by introducing new services and upgrades to the site.

One of the most significant new offerings in 2003 was called "Search Inside the Book," an expansion of the "Look Inside the Book" service that had been introduced two years earlier. While "Look Inside" allowed site visitors to see certain pages—the table of contents and the first chapter, for example—of selected books, the upgrade made most books listed on Amazon.com searchable by simple words or terms. A customer could either select a particular book from the 120,000 searchable titles and search inside it for specific words or phrases or search the entire site for books with the terms included. Although some publishers were concerned that the new technology would make it too easy for people to gain access to the content in their books without having to purchase them, many

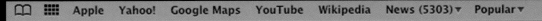
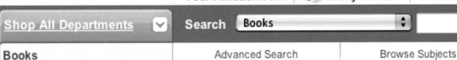

amazon.com   Hello. Sign in to get personalized recommendations. New customer? Start

Your Amazon.com | Today's Deals | Gifts & Wish Lists | Gift Ca

Shop All Departments ☑   Search   Books   ☀

Books   Advanced Search   Browse Subjects   New Re

The Great Gatsby and over 950,000 other

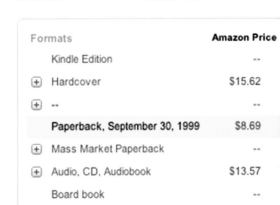

The Great Gatsby [Paperback]
F. Scott Fitzgerald ☑ (Author)

★★★☆ ☑ (1,301 customer reviews) | 👍 Like

List Price: $15.00

Price: $8.69 & eligible for FREE Super

You Save: $6.31 (42%)

In Stock.
Ships from and sold by **Amazon.com**. Gift-wrap

Want it delivered Wednesday, June 29? Order

165 new from $6.57   **703 used** from $1.76

Formats	Amazon Price
Kindle Edition	--
⊞ Hardcover	$15.62
⊞ --	--
Paperback, September 30, 1999	$8.69
⊞ Mass Market Paperback	--
⊞ Audio, CD, Audiobook	$13.57
Board book	--
⊞ Audible Audio Edition, Unabridged	$9.95 or

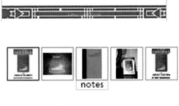

Click to LOOK INSIDE!

See all 9 customer images
Share your own customer images
Search inside this book

Amazon's "Look Inside" feature allowed online customers to "browse" a book before buying

were willing to cooperate with Amazon on the unique project.

In the first half of 2003, one title in particular attracted attention on Amazon .com: *Harry Potter and the Order of the Phoenix*, the fifth book in the popular *Harry Potter* series by author J. K. Rowling. Customers were able to place advance orders for the book starting on January 15. By the time it was officially released on June 21, more than 1.3 million copies had been pre-ordered worldwide—more than any other product in Amazon's eight-year history.

Strong sales of *Order of the Phoenix* helped Amazon post a profit for the third quarter of 2003. A fantastic holiday season and growth in international sales—by then, sites were live in six countries, including Canada, Japan, and France—combined with those sales to help the company realize its first full-year profit as well. Amazon reported earnings of $35 million for the year and promised to use that money to offer deeper discounts to its customers and to invest more dollars in technological advancements that would help distinguish it from competing "e-tailers," as online retailers had become known.

Amazon's relationship with Toys"R"Us came to an ugly end in 2004, when the toy store sued Amazon, saying the online store had not honored its agreement to make Toys"R"Us the exclusive toy and game seller on Amazon. (The lawsuit was eventually settled in 2009, when Amazon was ordered to pay Toys"R"Us $51 million.) In spite of that dispute, Amazon had a record year that was capped by its busiest holiday season yet. On a single day, more than 2.8 million items were ordered—an average of 32 per second—worldwide. At the end of the year, the company announced profits of $588 million.

That gave Bezos and his company much to celebrate the following year, when Amazon celebrated its 10th birthday with a party in Seattle that was broadcast live on the Amazon.com Web site. Comedian Bill Maher hosted the event, which was called "Show of Thanks," and musicians Bob Dylan and Norah Jones were among the featured performers. The company also thanked its loyal

Harry Potter and the Order of the Phoenix did huge business, selling more than 55 million copies in all

customers—more than 50 million people now visited the site monthly in the U.S. alone—by introducing Amazon Prime. The new feature provided free 2-day and discounted shipping for an annual fee of $79.

But as Amazon celebrated its success, financial analysts worried about the company's declining revenue. They were concerned that Amazon's prices were too low and that its free shipping option was eating into profits. During the first three months of 2005, for example, Amazon spent $167 million on shipping costs and received only a portion of that back from customers. The company was also investing heavily in its own team of computer programmers to perfect its search function and to tweak the site's features. And Amazon had increased its marketing budget, which was dedicated almost entirely to e-mail campaigns and promotions, by almost 30 percent in an effort to remain foremost in online shoppers' minds.

Bezos considered all those initiatives to be part of his big-picture growth plan that put customers first. He refused to worry publicly about the company's stock value going up or down. He wanted his employees to put customer service first instead of focusing on profits. "If we take care of customers, the stock will take care of itself in the long term," he said.

To prove his point, Bezos spent most of 2006 expanding the services, products, and features available through Amazon.com. By the end of the year, Amazon was offering online **digital** data storage to customers, a print-on-demand program for book publishers, and an online talk show in which host Bill Maher discussed books, music, and movies. In November, the company was voted number one in customer service in a national retail survey. December sales eclipsed all previous holiday sales records, thanks in large part to products such as Apple iPods and Nintendo Wii gaming systems. Even so, the company posted disappointing annual earnings of only $190 million, marking 2 straight years of declining profits.

> "It's possible to argue that Bezos didn't master much more than an evolution of commerce, replacing old-fashioned stores with a centralized sales and shipping center."
>
> JOSHUA COOPER RAMO, *TIME* MAGAZINE

Amazon's resilient growth impressed such business experts as *TIME* editor Joshua Cooper Ramo

The success of the *Harry Potter* series of fantasy books about a young wizard and his friends made British author J. K. Rowling a wealthy woman. It also helped make Amazon.com a profitable company and regularly set sales records on the site. When the fifth installment, *Harry Potter and the Order of the Phoenix*, was released in 2003, a record-setting 1.3 million copies were pre-ordered on Amazon. Two years later, when *Harry Potter and the Half-Blood Prince* was issued, Amazon received more than 1.5 million advance orders, another record. But when the seventh and final installment came out in 2007, that record was again shattered. Amazon delivered 2.2 million copies of *Harry Potter and the Deathly Hallows* to customers. "The anticipation for this book has been like none other in our history," said Greg Greeley, the company's vice president for books. "Customers are clearly excited about the book."

CHAPTER FIVE

Kindling for the Future

arly in 2007, Amazon's commitment to customer service and to the expansion of its product offerings paid off. Thanks largely to strong
sales of electronics and clothing, the company's profits rebounded. As many traditional retailers began pre-
dicting slower sales in the face of rising gas prices and
other economic pressures, Amazon was looking for-
ward to renewed growth instead.

One of the reasons Amazon was so optimistic about its future was a new product in the hopper: a portable electronic reader that would be able to **download**
digital books, **blogs**, magazines, and newspapers **wirelessly**. Similar products had
already been introduced by companies such as Sony, but Amazon had spent three
years perfecting the technology and developing a product that would go beyond
the experience competitors' readers offered. On November 19, 2007, Amazon released the Kindle—its first self-made product—at a price of $399. More than 90,000
digital books were immediately available for purchase, including almost all of the
current *New York Times* best sellers and new releases.

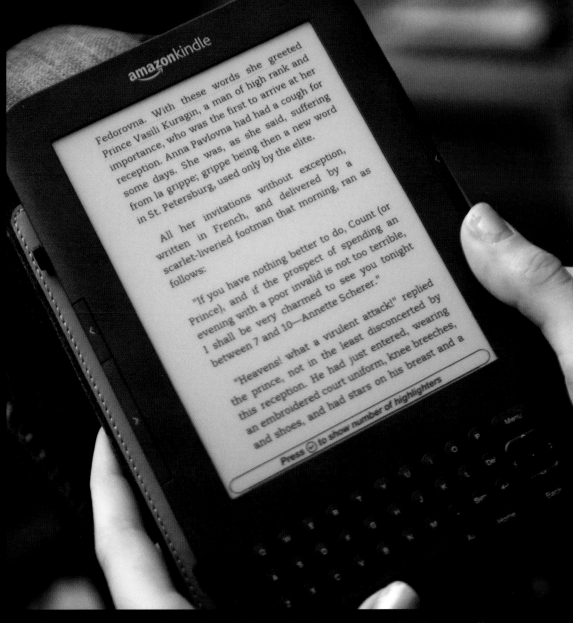

The Kindle's screen was designed to closely simulate the experience of reading type off paper

AMAZON.COM

A few of the earlier e-book devices had been almost as easy to read as the Kindle was, and some were similar in size (the Kindle's dimensions closely matched those of an actual paperback book). But none of the e-readers released prior to the Kindle included the ability to download books without connecting to a computer. That high-tech convenience seemed especially appealing to a younger audience. "The baby boomers have a love affair with paper," said novelist James Patterson when the Kindle was launched. "But the next-gen people, in their 20s and below, do everything on a screen."

Thanks to talk show host Oprah Winfrey, who promoted the Kindle on her television show, the device quickly became popular with both younger and older readers. Within a year of its launch, more than 250,000 Kindles had been sold, and by the fall of 2008, Amazon had reportedly sold out of the device due to heavy demand. Digital books accounted for 10 percent of Amazon's total book sales for the year, even though only 200,000 titles—just a fraction of the millions of books available on Amazon—were ready for download. Readers had clearly embraced the Kindle technology. "This is the most important thing we've ever done," Bezos said. "It's so ambitious to take something as highly evolved as the book and improve on it—and maybe even change the way people read."

The success of the Kindle helped Amazon push sales figures up during all of 2007, a trend that continued in 2008 as well. By 2009, when Amazon released an upgraded version of the Kindle to keep up with new e-readers released by Barnes & Noble and Sony, almost 400,000 digital books were available on the Web site. For the first time in company history, e-books sold better during the holiday shopping season than physical books. The day after Christmas, Amazon declared that the Kindle had become the "most gifted" item in the site's history.

Even as the Kindle quickly became the most popular item on Amazon.com, the company remained committed to expanding its services and products and to improving its customers' experiences. In 2009, it acquired online shoe and apparel retailer Zappos.com, introduced outdoor recreation products on the

site, and began its "Multi-Year Frustration-Free Packaging Initiative." For the initiative, Amazon teamed with such companies as Fisher-Price, Mattel, and Microsoft to streamline packaging and reduce the use of hard-to-open plastic clamshells and tightly wound wire ties securing items to packages. "I think we've all experienced the frustration that sometimes occurs when you try to get a new toy or electronics product out of its package," Bezos said. "It will take many years, but our vision is to offer our entire catalog of products in Frustration-Free Packaging."

By 2010, however, most of Amazon's advancements were related to the Kindle, including the January release of its third version—the Kindle DX. The new Kindle boasted global wireless capabilities, which allowed it to access the Internet anywhere, even in locations without wireless Internet service. Amazon also made Kindle **applications** available for smart phones, tablets, and personal computers. And the company's sales continued to soar.

Although Amazon remained tightlipped about its future product development plans, the company began expanding the workforce in its **hardware** division late in 2010, leading many observers to speculate that another Kindle-like device might be in the works. Some sources believed that music players would be an appropriate next venture because Amazon already had an inventory of albums and songs available online. The same could be said for a potential video player, since both television shows and movies were also available in a digital format on the site.

Whatever it does next, it's clear that Amazon's tradition of innovation will continue. Despite the doubts of some observers along the way, the company has grown from one of the first online stores to one of the largest retailers in the world, online or not. It's a good thing that early employees decided to abandon the beeping every time an order came in, or the company's Seattle headquarters would today be buzzing constantly.

"You have to give Jeff [Bezos] credit. His goal was to
turn Amazon into the Wal-Mart of the online world,
and, eureka, he's done it."

MARK R. ANDERSON, PUBLISHER OF
THE STRATEGIC NEWS SERVICE

TO THE MOON?

Jeff Bezos's entrepreneurial spirit led him to found Amazon.com in 1994. It also spurred another project that Bezos announced publicly in 2005: Blue Origin, a space travel venture with the ultimate goal of ferrying space tourists and scientists to and from outer space. Bezos, who became a billionaire after taking Amazon.com public in 1997, has provided much of the funding for the company's efforts to build a space vehicle that can take off and land vertically from a launch site in Texas. By 2006, the company had developed an egg-shaped test vehicle named *New Shepard*, but Blue Origin engineers warned that the final version of the rocket would likely not look the same. They also assured the press that the company wouldn't be offering sneak peeks of the vehicle. "The first time most of the public will see that vehicle," engineer Gary Lai said, "is when it's in the air and is flying."

GLOSSARY

PAGE 46

BUILT FOR SUCCESS

acquisitions purchases of companies by other companies

applications software programs designed to help a user perform tasks, play games, or take other action on a computer or computerized device

blogs online journals with regular written entries and comments from readers

brick-and-mortar describing businesses that operate an actual storefront, as opposed to those that operate online

circuit breaker an automatic device that stops the flow of electricity as a safety measure

comptroller a person who controls the finances of a company

digital recorded using a technique that converts text, sound, or images into electronic signals

download to transfer data to a computer system from a separate remote system, such as a Web site or e-mail service

economic having to do with the system of producing, distributing, and consuming goods within a society

engineers people who design or build computer systems (or other structures or machines) to solve problems

entrepreneur a person who organizes a new business venture and assumes the risks associated with it

feminist supporting activities or beliefs that favor equal rights and opportunities for women

hardware the physical components that make up a computer system or other computerized device

incorporated formed a firm or company into a corporation by completing all of the required procedures and paperwork

infringement an encroachment on or limitation of the rights of another person

marketing the process of promoting products or services

profit the amount of money that a business keeps after subtracting expenses from income

quarter one of four three-month intervals that together comprise the financial year; public companies must report certain data on a quarterly basis

revenue the money earned by a company; another word for income

search engine a computer program that finds and retrieves files or data from a computer network or the Internet based on search terms entered by a user

share one of the equal parts a company may be divided into; shareholders each hold a certain number of shares, or a percentage, of the company

software the programs that run a computer, or tell it how to operate

stock shared ownership in a company by many people who buy shares, or portions, of stock, hoping the company will make a profit and the stock value will increase

trust a bank account that holds money for a specific person or purpose and that is only made available under certain circumstances

wirelessly describing the sending and receiving of information over computer networks via radio signals instead of cables

SELECTED BIBLIOGRAPHY

Bilton, Nick. "Amazon Is Said to Look at Hardware beyond Kindle." *New York Times*, August 10, 2010. http://bits.blogs .nytimes.com/2010/08/10/amazon-hopes-to-build-hardware-beyond-kindle/?ref=amazon_inc.

Brooker, Katrina. "Beautiful Dreamer." *Fortune*, December 18, 2000.

Frey, Christine, and John Cook. "How Amazon.com Survived, Thrived and Turned a Profit." *Seattle Post-Intelligencer*, January 28, 2004.

Marcus, James. *Amazonia: Five Years at the Epicenter of the Dot.com Juggernaut*. New York: The New Press, 2004.

Ramo, Joshua Cooper. "1999 Person of the Year: Jeffrey P. Bezos." *TIME*, December 27, 1999.

Saunders, Rebecca. *Business the Amazon.com Way*. Oxford: Capstone Publishing Limited, 2001.

Spector, Robert. *Amazon.com: Get Big Fast*. New York: HarperBusiness, 2002.

INDEX

MAR 2013

CLIFTON PARK-HALFMOON PUBLIC LIBRARY, NY

0 00 06 04125831